HERRINGS
GO
ABOUT
THE SEA
IN
SHAWLS

HERRINGS GO ABOUT THE SEA IN SHAWLS

. . . and other classic howlers

from classrooms and

examination papers compiled

by Alexander Abingdon

{*originally titled* BONERS}

and illustrated by

DR. SEUSS

VIKING

VIKING
Published by the Penguin Group
Penguin Putnam Inc., 375 Hudson Street,
New York, New York 10014, U.S.A.
Penguin Books Ltd, 27 Wrights Lane,
London W8 5TZ, England
Penguin Books Australia Ltd, Ringwood,
Victoria, Australia
Penguin Books Canada Ltd, 10 Alcorn Avenue,
Toronto, Ontario, Canada M4V 3B2
Penguin Books (N.Z.) Ltd, 182–190 Wairau Road,
Auckland 10, New Zealand

Penguin Books Ltd, Registered Offices:
Harmondsworth, Middlesex, England

Published in 1997 by Viking Penguin,
a member of Penguin Putnam Inc.

3   5   7   9   10   8   6   4   2

Originally published under the title *Boners.*

LIBRARY OF CONGRESS CATALOGING-IN-PUBLICATION DATA
Herrings go about the sea in shawls: . . . and other classic howlers from
classrooms and examination papers / compiled by Alexander Abingdon and
illustrated by Dr. Seuss.
      p.   cm.
ISBN 0-670-87751-4 (alk. paper)
1. American wit and humor.   I. Abingdon, Alexander.
II. Seuss, Dr.
PN6231.B8H47   1997
818'.0208—dc21   97-21443

This book is printed on acid-free paper.
∞

Printed in the United States of America
Set in Fairfield Light
Designed by Brian Mulligan

FOREWORD

The feverish search for information grows apace. People are assuaging their thirst for boundless knowledge at the wells of synthetic waters. Learned and semi-learned purveyors of information are enriching—if not the reader—themselves, their families, their booksellers, and their publishers with volume after volume of closely packed and loosely gathered stores of knowledge.

It is with the keenest pleasure, therefore, that the editors of this particular book present an "Outline of Misinformation," a "Story of Errors," a "Symposium of Mistakes"—call it what you will. Here are no compilers of fat books on civilization, no tourists into the fallow fields of philosophy, no tracers of the outline of knowledge, only poor innocent harassed blunderers trying to find the right answers to the most uncivilized of mental tortures: the examination.

Out of the mouths of babes comes the material of this book—babes, at least, compared to their forbears among the Story-Tellers. Names have been omitted lest the authors of these treasures, many of whom are now undoubtedly millionaires and statesmen, motion picture actors and mechanical engineers, congressmen and customers' men—perhaps even presidents—should be embarrassed in their lofty positions by evidences of their youthful indiscretions.

In closing, or rather in opening to the pages that follow, let us tell a parable that might prompt you to temper a too harsh judgment on the mental sins of these young. A youngster arrived home from school with a garish "E" on his examination card. His mother demanded to see the questions that he had flunked so ignominiously. She read the examination paper carefully and turned on her child with a withering look, dismissing him with the comment: "You must be an absolute *marron*."

Editors Note, 1997:

Surveying the wreckage on the Information Interstate, we should have seen it coming, sixty-five years ago . . .

\

CONTENTS

HERRINGS GO ABOUT THE SEA IN SHAWLS

DEFINITIONS

Acrimony, sometimes called holy, is another name for marriage.

The Acropolis was the she-wolf that nursed Romeo and Juliet.

An adage is a thing to keep cats in.

Ali Baba means being away when the crime was committed.

Ambiguity means having two wives living at the same time.

Ambiguity means telling the truth when you don't mean to.

An antidote is a funny story that you have heard before.

An appendix is a portion of a book, which nobody yet has discovered of any use.

Explain the word "asset."

When you are making out an account you subtract the smaller from the larger amount. That is called assetaining the difference.

Average means something that hens lay eggs on.

A blizzard is the inside of a fowl.

What is a Blue Stocking?
A stocking that is blue instead of black or brown.
One who is a knight of the Garter.

A buttress is a woman who makes butter.—
W. R. H.

Celibacy is the crime a priest commits when he marries.—M. L. B.

Celibacy was a unit of land in the Mohamedan system.—M. L. B.

A claim letter states that something that was bought a while ago did not last as long as it was told it would and states the claim.

A brazier is the kind of garment
the Italians wore instead of
having their houses heated
by furnaces.

A compliment is when you say something to another which he and we know is not true.

A connoisseur is a person who stands outside a picture palace.

A deacon is the lowest kind of a Christian.

Doldrums are a series of high rocks near the Equator.

Double dealing is when you buy something wholesale to sell retail.

"Dour" means a sort of help, as in the hymn, "O God dour help in ages past."

An epistle is the wife of an apostle.

A Euphemism is a description of a disagreeable thing by an agreeable name. Example, the child is the father of the man.

Faith is that quality which enables us to believe what we know to be untrue.

The Feudal system was that if one man killed another, the man in the family of the murdered could kill the murderers.

A fugue is what you get in a room full of people when all the windows and doors are shut.

Genius is an infinite capacity for picking brains.

To germinate is to become a naturalized German.

The Dauphin was a rare fish that
used to inhabit the Arctic Circle
in the middle ages.

A gherkin is a native who runs
after people with a knife.

A goblet is a male turkey.—W. R. H.

A grass widow is the wife of a vegetarian.

Gravity is what you get when you eat too much and too fast.—B. M. CLARK

An heir is when anybody dies you get what is left.

What is an herbaceous border?
One who boards all the week and goes home on Saturdays and Sundays.

An invoice is another name for the conscience.

Isinglass is a whitish substance made from the bladders of surgeons.

Matrimony is a place where souls suffer for a time on account of their sins.

A Mayor is a he horse.

The letters M.D. signify "mentally deficient."

A miracle is something that someone does that cannot be done.

A momentum is what you give a person when they are going away.

A monologue is a conversation between two people, such as husband and wife.

Mussolini is a sort of material used for ladies' stockings.

An oboe is an American tramp.

An optimist is a man who looks after your eyes, a pessimist looks after your feet.

Oracles was the greatest orator of his day.
Orator was named after Oracles because he was the first orator.

A protoplasm is a person who is always prophesying.

The Papal Bull was a mad bull kept by the Pope in the Inquisition to trample on Protestants.

The Papal Bull was really a cow that was kept at the Vatican to supply milk for the Pope's children.

Paraffin is the next order of angels above seraphims.

A period is a dot at the end of a sentence.
Period costumes are dresses all covered with dots.

A polygon is a man who has many wives.

A polygon is a dead parrot.

Posters are sheets of paper pasted on black-guards.

A prism is a kind of dried plum, because people say "prunes and prisms."

A prodigal is the son of a priest.

The oracle told Laius that if he
had a son, it would kill
him.—E. A.

A Prostestant is a woman who gets her living through an immortal life.

A refugee keeps order at a football match.

Revolution is a form of government abroad.

Sans-culottes—That class of people in France who wore no breeches.—L. E. E.

Scent is the sound made by hounds.

A Senator is half horse and half man.

A sinecure is a disease without a cure.

A skeleton is a man with his inside out and his outside off.

S.O.S. is a musical term meaning same only softer.

A Soviet is a cloth used by waiters in hotels.

The Sphinx are some people that live in the Phillipine Islands.

A spinster is a bachelor's wife.

The Stoics were the disciples of Zero, and believe in nothing.

The Supreme Cort is our country's cort. It consists of 1 chief justic and 8 sociable justic. What they say goes.

Transparent means something you can see through, for instance a keyhole.

A vacuum is an empty space where the Pope lives.

LITERATURE AND THE ARTS

Sir Toby was Olivia's uncle, but otherwise he was no relation to her.

Milton's poetry is full of Biblical illusions.

Tennyson wrote a poem called "Grave's Energy."

Epics describe the brave deeds of men called epicures.

George Eliot left a wife and children to mourn his genii.

Write a sentence showing clearly the meaning of "posterity."

He had a cat, but nothing else lived on his posterity.

The man looked as if he had been reduced to posterity.

Henry pade the fare because of his posterity.

By his clothes he seemed a person of great posterity.

The cat leaped about and then sat on its posterity.

Cassius was a vile selfish man who was always doing his best to make his own ends meet.

Lord Macaulay suffered from gout and wrote all his poems in iambic feet.

What do you know of King Arthur?
King Arthur collected all the fine brave good-looking young men of his time and called them The Knuts of the Round Table.

Shakespeare lived at Windsor with his merry wives.

In conclusion we may say that Shylock was greedy, malicious, and indeed, entirely viscous.

From an essay on Shakespeare:
There are some passages in Shakespeare's work, which are quite pretty, as "Spoil the rod, and bare the child," and lots of others.

Homer was not written by Homer but by another man of that name.

Shakespeare wrote tragedies, comedies and errors.

An epitaph is a short sarcastic poem.

Tennyson wrote a most beautiful poem called, "In Memorandum."

Who sang, "Come unto these yellow sands"? These sounds were made in the air by Aerial.

Bassanio sang a beautiful song called, "Tell me, where is fancy bread?"

From an essay:
I stood on the cliff, the sea was ruff and the wind roard and not a sole was to be seen.

Polonius was
a mythical sausage.

King Arthur was a person who was washed up when a baby, and Merlin said it should be so and they proved it.

Poetry is a thing you make prose of.

Shakespeare wrote the Merry Widow.

Samuel Johnson was known as the Doctor of Divinity because he wrote the first dictionary.

Homer wrote the Oddity.

Most of Shakespeare's plays were terrible tragedies.

Pope wrote principally in heroic cutlets.

Describe the figure of speech or artifice of style used in the following: "The child is father to the man."

Answer: "This was written by Shakespeare. He often made this kind of mistake."

Of Charles Lamb:

It was his sister and him who essayed most of Shakespeare's writings.

Another: It was Mary Lamb with Charles who between them wrote most of Shakespeare's fairy tales.

Describing Tom Sawyer (Mark Twain): He was a smart looking boy, very fond of fighting, and he was always sharp at this kind of job. His character was always good sometimes.

"Essays of Elia": The attempts of Elijah to get food.

Write a sentence showing clearly the meaning of "asterisk."

Last night my father got drunk and made an asterisk out of himself.

The "Complete Angler" is another name for Euclid because he wrote all about angles.

Wells' history is a veritable millstone on the road to learning.

Milton wrote "Paradise Lost"; then his wife died and he wrote "Paradise Regained."

Keats is a poet who wrote on a greasy urn.

Robert Burns had one son who was called Wha Hae.

"The Lark that soars on dewy
wing" means that the lark was
going so high and flapping his
wings so hard that he broke
into prespiration.

Poetry is when every line begins with a capital letter.

Prospero is the clown in "The Vicar of Wakefield," by Dickens.

Virgil was the mother of Christ.

A morality play is a play in which the characters are goblins, ghosts, virgins and other supernatural creatures.

Contrary to most of the great poets and authors, Milton's life was pure for he was neither a great drinker or an opium-eater.

Lady Macbeth died of the sleeping sickness.

Keats believed in the immorality of Beauty.

The theme of this poem is that Longfellow shot an arrow into the air, and many years afterward he found it in the heart of a friend.

Name three tragedies by Shakespeare.
Macbeth, King Lear, and Twelve Nights in a Bar Room.

The opening sentence from a student's theme on "My First Affair of the Heart":
"She was the positive symposium of pulchritude."

Definition of a medieval mystery play:
A play in which the person guilty of murder is not discovered until the final curtain.

Her body was one of a very strong physique but enclosed in it was a large tender heart filled with effection for children.

I had an ample teacher last term. He taught us to do three things. First how to write briefs and then to exaggerate them; second how to extract substances from novels, and last how to interrupt poetry.

Horace wrote odes and odesseys.

Chaucer was a great English poet who wrote many poems and verses and sometimes wrote literature.

The Song of Roland was, my country oh! how sweet it seems to me.

Milton wrote Paradise Lost and was a Roman Catholic who graduated at Oxford. He also had a good education.

"The Passing of Arthur" is a beautiful poem. It reminds me a lot of "Custer's Last Stand."

Humor was then introduced into the English drama—for example, a wife wringing her husband's neck.

Penelope was the last hardship that Ulysses endured on his journey.

"And doth not Brutus bootless kneel?" means Brutus knelt without his boots on.

When Adam Bede was an old man he entered a convent and became the father of English Literature.

A poetic license is a license you get from the Post Office to keep poets. You get one also if you want to keep a dog. It costs two dollars and you call it a dog license.

As well as real actors and actresses there are those who we go to see for charity. These are called immature.

The dome of St. Paul's is supported by eight peers, all of which are unfortunately cracked.

Michael Angelo painted the dome of the Sistine Madonna.

An interval in music is the distance from one piano to the next.

Mandolines are high officials in China.

Gainsborough painted
Mrs. Siddons as a tragic mouse.

Andrea del Sarto was not quarrelsome, while his wife was of the opposite sex.

Contralto is a low sort of music that only ladies sing.

Syncopation is emphasis on a note that is not in the piece.

BIBLE, RELIGIONS, MYTH

In Christianity a man can only have one wife. This is called Monotony.

Laud was a very high-minded man, and thought that every priest should wear vespers and they could expect something if they didn't.

The message came to Abraham that he should bear a son, and Sarah, who was listening behind the door, laughed.

Job had one trouble after another. He lost all his cattle and all his children and then he had to go and live alone with his wife in the desert.

Why was John the Baptist beheaded?
For dancing too persistently with the daughter of Herodotus.

In what order do the Gospels come?
One after the other.

The Great Flood was sent because of the large numbers of dirty people.

From a Catechism question:
. . . to love, honour and suckle my Father and Mother.

If any man smite thee on the right cheek, smite him on the other also.

The greatest miracle in the Bible is when Joshua told his son to stand still and he obeyed him.

Who was sorry when the Prodigal Son returned?
The fatted calf.

The saints are classified so that their be one for each kind of human traits, as shipwreck, childbirth, etc.

Abraham was the father of Lot and had ten wives. One was called Hismale, and the other Hagar. He kept one at home and the other he sent into the desert where she became a pillow of salt in the daytime and a pillow of fire by night.

John the Baptist was a centuar which means that he was half a man and half a horse. It says his head was on a charger.

Lazarus used to eat the food out of the rich man's stable.

The Tower of Babel was the place where Solomon kept his wives.

The Mosaic Law was a law compelling people to have their floors laid with coloured stones.

The Pharisies were bad people who used to wash.

Cornelius was the first Gentile virgin.

Solomon had 300 wives
and 700 porcupines.

Jacob was a patriarch who brought up his twelve sons to be patriarchs, but they did not take to it.

Jacob didn't eat much, as a rule, except when there was a famine in the land.

Esau was a man who wrote fables and sold his copyright for a mess of potash.

Abraham, after the sacrifice of Isaac, called the place Rio Janeiro.

The first book in the Bible is Guinessis.

The Bible is against bigamy when it says that no man can serve two masters.

Whenever David played to Saul the latter kept a javelin handy.

Eliza came before the King wrapped in a camel's hair, and said: "Behold me, I am Eliza the Tit-bit."

Gomorrah was Sodom's wife. They were both destroyed by brimstone and treacle, and Lot had to flee with them.

When David slew Goliath with a catapult the age of missile warfare commenced. This incident drove the first nail into the coffin of Feudalism.

If David had one fault it was a slight tendency to adultery.

Little is known of the prophet Elijah, except that he once went for a cruise with a widow.

Sarah was Abraham's half-wife, otherwise mid-wife, sometimes called columbine.

A certain man drew his bow
at a venture, but missed the
venture and hit Ahab.

Thomas Crammer was a college student who translated the old Testiment into the new one.

Before a man could become a monk he had to have his tonsils cut.

Christianity was introduced into Britain by the Romans in 55 B.C.

Justinian was the name given to a group of Christian friars, whose patron saint was Saint Justine.

Moses was the crucified son of Christ.

Those who did not accept the Orthodox faith were hereditary.

In the days of Joseph the Egyptians gave refuse to the Israelites.

Ordeals were the bones of saints. They were used to swear an oath upon.

The Wesleyan movement started when the native sultan of the part of India called Wesley tried to get Calcutta. The intention was to stop the commerce of English in that section. The natives were defeated and the Great Mogul killed.

The evils of Mohammedanism were that they believed in thirst and Mohammed was only a lesser profit.

Budda is worshipped chiefly in Budda Pest.

The gods of the Indians are chiefly Mohammed and Buddha and in their spare time they do a lot of carving.

Aladdin was a man who had a ring, and every time he rang a Guinness sprang out of the ground.

Baccus first taught the Greeks to get drunk.

Medusa was a famous Gorgon and a Frenchman named Zola wrote a book about her.

Another well-known Greek God was Appolinaris.

Charon was the man who fried soles over the sticks.

Achilles was the boy whose
mother dipped him in the
River Stinx until he was
intollerable.

Theseus begged Minos to try and kill the labrynth.

Plato was the god of the Underground.

The Gorgons were three sisters that lived in the islands of the Hesperides somewhere in the Indian Ocean. They had long snakes for hair, tusks for teeth, and claws for nails, and they looked like women only more horrible.

GEOGRAPHY

Asked to name six animals peculiar to the Arctic regions, a boy replied: "Three bears and three seals."

Grade school pupil who was asked why the Panama Canal would aid in the defense of the country in time of war said: "The locks will keep out the enemy's ships."

Australia sends to England wine made from a bird called the Emu.

Climate lasts all the time, but weather only a few days.

Latitude tells you how hot you are, and longitude how cold you are.

The Menai Sraits are crossed by a tubercular bridge.

Sienna is famous for being burnt.

The climate of Bombay is such that its inhabitants have to live elsewhere.

The sun never sets on the British Empire because the British Empire is in the East and the sun sets in the West.

The trade of Spain is small, owing to the insolence of the people.

The Esquimaux are God's frozen people.

The sun sets in the west and hurries round to the east to be in time to rise the next morning.

The people in Iceland are Equinoxes.

Name three animals peculiar to the frigid region.

The lion, the giraffe and the elephant would be *peculiar* to the frigid region, but the polar bear, the seal, and the walrus live there.

People go to Africa to hunt rhinostriches.

Glaciers spread a murrain over the land.

The highest peak in the alps is Blanc Mange.

The Arctic regions are neither hot nor cold, they abound in birds of beautiful plumage and of no song such as the elephant and the camel.

Children have hook worm in the tropical regions.

An axis is an imaginary line on which the earth is supposed to take a daily routine.

The equator is a menagerie lion running round the earth and through Africa.

Imports are ports very far inland.

Nearly at the bottom of Lake Michigan is Chicago.

The chief occupation of the inhabitants of Perth is dying.

The Rhine is boarded by wooden mountains.

The inhabitants of Moscow are called Mosqui-toes.

The Pyramids are a range of mountains be-tween France and Spain.

The Eskimoes hardly have any wives at all.

Georgia was settled by thieves and animals taken from the English jail.

A mountain range is a cooking stove used at high altitudes.

An Indian reservation consists of a mile of land for every five square Indians.

The only signs of life in the Tundras are a few stunted corpses.

Among the islands of the West Indies are the Pyjamas, noted for toilet sponges.

Fiume is the name of a mountain in Japan.

The whole world, except the United States, lies in the temperate zone.

The people of India are divided into casts and outcasts.

Norway's capital is called Christianity.

Lipton is the capital of Ceylon.

The Nile is full of crocodiles and pyramids.

The population of London is a bit too thick.

China is called China because the first china was made there.

Persian cats is the chief industry of Persia, hence the word "purr."

The North Sea is also called the German Ocean, but they don't really think it is.

England is located on the coast of Great Britain not far from the sea, which makes good fishing.

The Mediterranean and the Red Sea are connected by the sewage canal.

New York stands on the Atlantic sideboard.

The Arctic circle is the circle in the Arctic region where it is day all day long.

New York is behind Greenwich time because America was not discovered until very much later.

Certain areas of Egypt are cultivated by irritation.

Vesuvius is a volcano and if you
will climb up to the top you will
see the creator smoking.

The Poles must be 90° from the Equator, therefore they are north and south, because if they were east and west they couldn't be.

Zanzibar is noted for its monkeys. The British Governor lives there.

A water shed is a shed in the middle of the sea where ships shelter during a storm.

Melba—where Napoleon was imprisoned.

The Rialto was the business end of Venus.

SCIENCE AND MATHEMATICS

Science is material. Religion is immaterial.

If there was no nitrogen in the air we should die of fits of laughter.

Name the three races of man.
Foot race, horse race and automobile race.

Charles Darwin was a natulist who wrote the Organ of the Spices.

Huxley was the greatest antagonist of the nineteenth century.

A planet is a body of earth surrounded by sky.

The solid wastes are excreted through the retina.

The left lung is smaller than the right one because the soul is located near there.

Benjamin Franklin produced
electricity by rubbing cats
backward.

The spinal column is a bunch of bones down your back to show feeling.

The theory of evolution was greatly objected to because it made men think.

The scientific name of the flea is hegira. It was given that name by Mohammet when he went to Mecca.

A grasshopper has three pair of wings—anterior, posterior and bacteria.

A grasshopper passes through all the life stages from infancy to adultery.

The law of gravity was enacted by the British Parliament.

The dog came bounding down the path emitting whelps at every bound.

Three kinds of blood vessels are arteries, veins and caterpillars.

The cow gives us milk. A young cow is called a calf and gives us jelly.

The cuckoo is a bird that lays other bird's eggs in its own nest and "viva voce."

A focus is a thing like a mushroom, but if you eat it you will feel differently from a mushroom, for focusses is poison.

Mushrooms always grow in damp places and so they look like umbrellas.

Rhubarb is a kind of celery gone bloodshot.

The pineapple is the fruit of the pine tree.

If anyone should faint in church put her head between the knees of the nearest medical man.

The principal parts of the eye are the pupil, the moat, and the beam.

A cat is a quadruped, the legs, as usual, being at the four corners.

To keep milk from turning sour you should keep it in the cow.

To pinch a butterfly you pinch its borax.

The zebra is like the horse only striped, and is chiefly used to illustrate the letter Z.

The dodo is a bird that is nearly decent now.

When you stroke a cat by drawing your hand along its back it cocks its tail up like a ruler, so as you can't get no further.

Respiration is composed of two acts, first inspiration and then expectoration.

Man is the only animal who can strike a light.

Quinine is the bark of a tree: canine is the bark of a dog.

The animal which possess the greatest attachment for man is woman.

A sure-footed animal is an animal that when it kicks it does not miss.

A thermometer is an instrument for raising temperance.

Gravity was discovered by Isaac Walton. It is chiefly noticeable in the autumn, when the apples are falling off the trees.

The process of turning steam into water again is called Conversation.

To remove air from a flask, fill the flask with water, tip the water out, and put the cork in quick.

A vacuum is a U-tube with a flask at one end.

Herrings go about
the sea in shawls.

Chlorine gas is very injurious to the human body, and the following experiments should, therefore, only be performed on the teacher.

A litre is a nest of young puppies.

Water is composed of two gins. Oxygin and Hydrogin. Oxygin is pure gin, Hydrogin is gin and water.

The difference between air and water is that air can be made wetter, but water cannot.

A magnet is a thing you find in a bad apple.

Ammonium chloride is also called silly maniac.

Our school is ventilated by hot currants.

To fill an apparatus with acidulated water, turn on the taps and acidulate.

Explain the meaning of "erg."
When people are playing football and you want them to do their best you erg them on.

The probable cause of earthquakes may be attributed to bad drainage and neglect of sewage.

The tides are a fight between the earth and the moon. All water tends towards the moon, because there is no water in the moon, and nature abhors a vacuum. Gravitation at the earth keeps the water rising all the way to the moon. I forget where the sun joins in this fight.

Three states of water are high water, low water, and break water.

Define the elements.
Mustard, pepper, salt and vinegar.

The earth makes a resolution every twenty-four hours.

In some rocks there are to be found the fossil footprints of fishes.

Polyps swim about the sea when they are young and when they get old they fasten themselves on their relations and live like that for the rest of their lives.

To collect fumes of sulphur, hold a deacon over a flame in a test tube.

Nitrogen is not found in Ireland because it is not found in a free state.

The cuckoo does not lay
its own eggs.

A therm is a germ that creeps into the gas meter and causes rapid consumption.

Typhoid fever may be prevented by fascination.

When you breathe you inspire. When you do not breathe you expire.

All brutes are imperfect animals. Man alone is a perfect beast.

Henry Ford invented perpetual motion.

A man has x miles to travel. He goes a miles by train, b miles by boat, and c miles he walks. The rest he cycles. How far does he cycle?

$d, e, f, g, h, i, j, k, l, m, n, o, p, q, r, s, t, u, v, w$ miles.

Parallel lines never meet unless you bend one or both of them.

A parallel straight line is one that when produced to meet itself does not meet.

Define a circle.
Take your center and take your distance and draw a straight curved line. This is a circle and all lines drawn to it are equal.

A circle is a round line with no kinks in it, joined up so as not to show where it began.

Two straight lines cannot enclose a space unless they are crooked.

Algebra was the wife of Euclid.

When a graph of "y equals x^2" is plotted, what is the resultant curve?

An eclipse.

Isosceles triangles are used on maps to join up places with the same weather.

Things which are equal to each other are equal to anything else.

Algebraical symbols are used when you do not know what you are talking about.

The logarithm of a given number is the number of times the given number must be squared in order that the given number may be equal to this number.

An axiom is a thing that is so visible that it is not necessary to see it.

Geometry teaches us
to bisex angels.

A circle is a line which meets its other end without ending.

A polygon with seven sides is called a hooligan.

HISTORY

Caesar was borned July 12, 100 B.C. he was a great general and a great orator he was well up on his Greek and art. His mother taught him when he was a young boy. He held his first office at the age of thirteen. He fought in many battles. The Ides of March murdered him because they thought he was going to be made king.

Caesar extinguished himself on the battlefields of Gaul.

The Augustan era was a mistake of Augustus.

Attila was the wife of Justinian, and was a great help to him.

Pepsin was king of the Franks.

In the Middle Ages the Pope had very great sexual powers.

Medieval commerce was carried on chiefly in Venus. She sent her sailors all over the world.

Describe the hardships of the Crusaders on their way to the Holy Land.

Many of them died of salvation.

The wife of Columbus was Columbine.

Joan of Arc was cannonised by Bernard Shaw.

Martin Luther was nailed to the church door at Wittenburg for selling papal indulgences.

Martin Luther died a horrible death. He was excommunicated by a bull.

Catherine of Medsi was for breaking away from the Catholic Church but St. Botholomew issued a bill against it and was carried out. This still held the people under the Roman Catholic Church.

Jean Rousseau: a Frenchman who believed in letting nature take its course. He was against the advancement of civilization. He wrote a book, Society Combat.

Watchword of the French Revolution: Liberty, Equality and Maternity.

The Romans made their roads straight so that the Britons should not hide round the corners.

Give King Alfred's views on modern life had he been alive today.

If Alfred had survived to the present day he would be such an exceedingly old man that his views on any subject would be quite worthless.

William the Conqueror fitted out some vessels and marched across the land.

After the great feasts, William I used to entertain the barons by letting off fireworks.

Next in rank to the overlord were the beeves.

King Richard was captured and put in prison by the German Emperor, but the English people were very fond of their ruler, so they boiled him out.

Magna Charta said that the King was not to order taxis without the consent of Parliament.

Edward III would have been King of France if his mother had been a man.

The conquest of Ireland began in 1170 and is still going on.

Henry VIII had an abbess
on his knee, which made
walking difficult.

Henry V was rather a good king, only like many other kings he often went mad.

Henry VIII married Catherine of Aragon. He soon grew tired of her and divorced and beheaded her. He next married Anne Boleyn and also beheaded her. He then married Anne of Cleves and beheaded her—and so on.

Wolsey saved his life by dying on the way from York to London.

Henry VIII was very luxurious. He had six wives—Anne Boleyne was one. When he met her first he flung his handkerchief at her. When he married her the Pope sent him a bull. It drove him into the Protestant Church. Anne Boleyne gave birth to Queen Elizabeth. After her confinement in the Tower, Harry had her beheaded as he wanted to be a widower again.

Philip had made England Roman Catholic, but when Elizabeth came to the throne England was made Christian.

Queen Elizabeth was the "Virgin Queen." As a queen she was a success.

The Spanish Armada was where that there was many people without work and it got to be where there were more and more getting without work and was going around begging and the queen tried to stop it but she found that she couldn't and she had them captured and beheaded.

Queen Elizabeth was the Roses, and, fearing that Mary, Queen of Scots, would marry her husband, Sir Walter Raleigh, she beheaded her and in remorse sent Raleigh to discover the United States. When he returned without doing so he was executed by Elizabeth's son, James I, after gaining time to write his long and varied biography in the Tower.

Drake was playing bowls when he was told the invisible armada was in sight.

The ancestors of the English people were Queen Elizabeth and Cardinal Woolsey.

Queen Elizabeth rode through Coventry with nothing on, and Raleigh offered her his cloak.

James the First claimed the throne through his grandfather because he had no father.

Raleigh died in James I's reign and started smoking.

Cromwell was the executor of Charles I.

They gave William IV a lovely funeral. It took six men to carry the beer.

The people didn't like King James II and after three years they decomposed him.

William III, on his way to Hampton Court, stumbled over a mole and broke his collar stud—which was fatal to a man of his constituency.

A lot of Englishmen were shut up in the Black Hole of Calcutta with one small widow. Only four got out alive.

Queen Victoria was the longest queen on the throne.

The Battle of Trafalgar was fought on sea, therefore it is sometimes called Waterloo.

In 1658 the Pilgrims crossed the ocean and this was known as Pilgrims Progress.

The Duck of Wellington won a big battle and when he finished he had one arm and one eye and he looked through the telescope with his blind eye and said it was alright and that is how he won the battle.

The Prodigal Fathers sailed for the New World in 1620.

Where was the Declaration of Independence signed?

At the bottom.

Explain what Cleveland meant by "a public office is a public trust."

A trust is a "conspiracy in restraint of trade." Therefore a public office is a conspiracy to restrain trade.

Louis XVI was gelatined during
the French Revolution.

Let us compare the Constitution to a boat with Washington, James Madison and the several others fishing from it with the states as fishes. Some of these little suckers got hooked right off but New York and Virginia, the bass, put up a hard fight in which Patrick Henry took Virginia's part against James Madison. Patrick Henry won but the line was too strong and he along with Virginia came aboard. New York was caught easily and only Rhode Island remained. She would not be caught so they threatened to dynamite the pool, that is, to treat her as a foreign country, so she bit and the thirteen states stood a "New Nation under God."

Horace Greeley was the worst defeated candidate ever elected.

The President has a cabinet in order to keep his china in it.

Mr. Million is Secretary of the Treasury.

The chief executive of Massachusetts is the electric chair.

Armistice Day is celebrated each year to perpetuate the Great War.

LANGUAGE ARTS

Gender shows whether a man is masculine, feminine, or neuter.

An injection is a shout or scream raised by a person too surprised or frightened to make a sentence with his thoughts. It is not quite a human language. The lower animals say nothing else but injections. Accordingly ill-natured and cross people by their injections come very near to beasts.

A conjunction is a place where two railway lines meet.

An abstract noun is one that cannot be heard, seen, touched, or smelt.

An interjection is a sudden explosion of mind.

A proposition is for a country to have no alcolic drinks in it.

A sentence that does not depend on any word in the sentence is not subordinate but inordinate.

Give an example of collective noun.
Garbage-can.

A metaphor is a thing you shout through.

Gender is the destruction of sex.

When a word gets out of date it is termed "dead" and so gradually a language is built up.

No is the adverb of negotiation.

Put the following words in a sentence—bliss, happiness.
O bliss, O happiness!

The future of "I give" is "You take."

A passive verb is when the subject is the sufferer, as "I am loved."

Degrees of comparison of "Bad."
Bad: very sick: dead.

The masculine of vixen is vicar.

Masculine, man; feminine, woman; neuter, corpse.

Feminines: Bear, vixen; Sheep, you. Masculine of ladybird: The masculine of ladybird sounds as if it ought to be gentlemanbird, but that looks funny.

The feminine of bachelor is lady in waiting.

The plural of forget-me-not is forget-us-not.

The plural of ox is oxygen.

Define the first person.
Adam.

Give the passive of "John shot my dog."
"My dog shot John."

The opposite of evergreen is nevergreen.

Correct "It was me who broke the window."
"It wasn't me who broke the window."

What is the last letter of the English alphabet?
Yours truly.

Habeas Corpus was a phrase used during the great plague of London, and means "Bring out your dead."

Gallia omnis est divisa in partes tres.
All Gaul is quartered into three halves.

De mortuis nil nisi bonum.
There's nothing but bones in the dead.

Pascebatque suas quisque senator oves.
Every senator used to live on his own eggs.

Timeo Danaos et dona ferentes.
J'estime les Danois et leur dents de fer.

Dido vento reditura secundo.
Dido will come again with her second wind.

Pax in bello.
Freedom from indigestion.

Ave Domine.
Lord, I am a bird.

Agnus Dei.
A woman composer famous for her church music.

LXXX.
Love and kisses.

A.D.
All dates after Christ or anteduluvian.

Hors d'oeuvre.
Out of work.

Hors de combat.
War horse.

Notre voisin est mort d'une congestion pulmonaire.
Our neighbour died in a crush on a Pullman car.

Mes souvenirs sont pen précis.
My recollections are precious few.

Voici l'Anglais avec son sangfroid habituel.
Here comes the Englishman with his usual
bloody cold.

Le peuple ému répondit.
The purple emu laid another egg.

Très volontiers, répondit-il.
Three volunteers responded.

MISCELLANEOUS

My brother was kicked because he was wicked in the seat of his pants.

When Bismarck died his brains were examined and he proved to have been the most intellectual man of his time.

She was a lion in front and a dragon in the rear.

Our forefathers are not living as long as they did.

Seafaring men in the habit of drinking are liable to collide with other vessels.

Queen Victoria said "we are not much amused" when she went to the pantomime with Prince Concert.

A deacon is a mass of inflammable material placed in a prominent position to warn the people.

Writ of Habeas Corpus means a man is not allowed to commit adultery without permission of the court.

The serfs were attached to the
soil and when it moved, they
moved with it.

Letters in sloping type are in hysterics.

When a lady and a gentleman are walking on the foot-path the lady should walk inside the gentleman.

Lord Mayors of London are famous city men who are generally benighted.

The Prince of Wales uses a different title when he travels in the Congo.

The shop windows looked very gay; lump sugar, granulated, and castor were arranged in different coloured bowls according to their sex.

The jockey lost two of his teeth when his horse fell, and had to be destroyed.

The theory of exchange, as I understand it, is not very well understood.

The Pilgrim Fathers were Adam and Eve.

M. Poincaré is known by his saying "Every day and in every way I get it better and better."

Where are the Kings of England crowned?
On their heads.

Queen Elizabeth was a vurgin queen, and she was never marrid. She was so fond of dresses that she was never seen without one on. She was beautefull and clever with a red hed and freckles.

Henry said, "Beware of the Brides of March."

During the Napoleonic Wars crowned heads were trembling in their shoes.

Teacher's dictation: "His choler rose to such a height that passion well nigh choked him."

Pupil's reproduction: "His collar rose to such a height that fashion well nigh choked him."

The wife of a duke is a ducky.

When we got there our trunk hadn't arrived, so we had to sleep in something else.

Socrates died from an overdose of wedlock.

False doctrine means giving people the wrong medicine.

Her mother, being immortal, had died.

Always choose a good neighbour, and if you are lucky enough to get a bath, have it at once.

There are only two crimes visited with capital punishment, murder and suicide.

Everybody needs a holiday from one year's end to another.

The Press today is the mouth-organ of the people.

Big Bill Thompson is America's Mustard King.

The King was crowned in the Crystal Palace with his sepulchre in his hand.

The first man who went to the Crusades was Robinson Crusoe.

The most interesting feature
of the zoo was the largest
ape in capacity.

Lord Bacon was impeached for deceiving brides.

The Emperor of Japan is called the Mikado, but no one has seen him since the Middle Ages.

In the United States people are put to death by elocution.

A democracy believes in God and a republic doesn't.

The form of government most commonly used in the cities is keep to the right.

One argument for the abolition of the jury system is that it costs too much to buy chairs and to hire a room for them.

Certainly the pleasures of youth are great, but they are nothing to the pleasures of adultery.

A man who marries twice commits bigotry.

Most bulls are harmless, but cows stare horribly.

A phlegmatic person is one who has chronic broncitis.

The different kinds of senses are commonsense and nonsense.